CELEBRATING HOLIDAYS

Halloween

by Rachel Grack

BLASTOFF!
2
READERS

BELLWETHER MEDIA • MINNEAPOLIS, MN

Note to Librarians, Teachers, and Parents:

Blastoff! Readers are carefully developed by literacy experts and combine standards-based content with developmentally appropriate text.

Level 1 provides the most support through repetition of high-frequency words, light text, predictable sentence patterns, and strong visual support.

Level 2 offers early readers a bit more challenge through varied simple sentences, increased text load, and less repetition of high-frequency words.

Level 3 advances early-fluent readers toward fluency through increased text and concept load, less reliance on visuals, longer sentences, and more literary language.

Level 4 builds reading stamina by providing more text per page, increased use of punctuation, greater variation in sentence patterns, and increasingly challenging vocabulary.

Level 5 encourages children to move from "learning to read" to "reading to learn" by providing even more text, varied writing styles, and less familiar topics.

Whichever book is right for your reader, Blastoff! Readers are the perfect books to build confidence and encourage a love of reading that will last a lifetime!

This edition first published in 2018 by Bellwether Media, Inc.

No part of this publication may be reproduced in whole or in part without written permission of the publisher. For information regarding permission, write to Bellwether Media, Inc., Attention: Permissions Department, 5357 Penn Avenue South, Minneapolis, MN 55419.

Library of Congress Cataloging-in-Publication Data

Names: Koestler-Grack, Rachel A., 1973- author.
Title: Halloween / by Rachel Grack.
Description: Minneapolis, MN : Bellwether Media, Inc., 2018. | Series: Blastoff! Readers: Celebrating Holidays | Includes bibliographical references and index. | Audience: Grades K-3. | Audience: Ages 5-8.
Identifiers: LCCN 2016052725 (print) | LCCN 2017012618 (ebook) | ISBN 9781626176218 (hardcover : alk. paper) | ISBN 9781681033518 (ebook)
Subjects: LCSH: Halloween–Juvenile literature.
Classification: LCC BF1572.H35 (ebook) | LCC BF1572.H35 K64 2018 (print) | DDC 394.2646–dc23
LC record available at https://lccn.loc.gov/2016052725

Editor: Christina Leighton.   Designer: Lois Stanfield

Printed in the United States of America, North Mankato, MN.

Table of Contents

Halloween Is Here!

Children are dressed in scary and funny costumes. They go from door to door to collect candy.

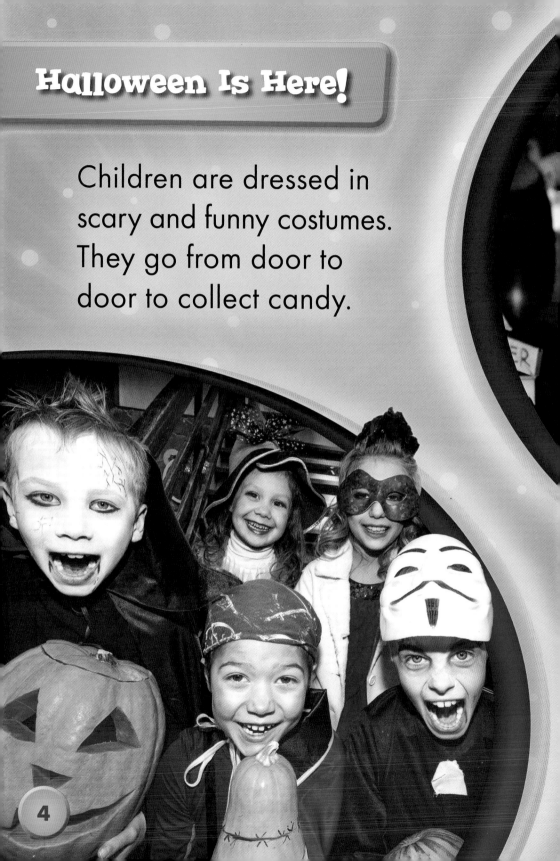

Homes are decorated with ghosts
and skeletons. It is Halloween!

Halloween is a spooky holiday in October.

Children and adults celebrate by dressing up and eating candy. Halloween brings people together!

Who Celebrates Halloween?

Halloween is celebrated around the world. The holiday became popular in the United States in the 1800s.

Halloween in France

Halloween fair
in Amsterdam

Many places in Europe
and Australia have their
own **traditions**.

Halloween Beginnings

Samhain in
Edinburgh, Scotland

Halloween began as a **Celtic** holiday called *Samhain*.

The **festival** marked the end of summer. People wore masks and set out treats for ghosts.

Celtic Region Map

Europe

◯ Celtic Region

Christians turned Samhain into All Hallows' Day to honor **saints**.

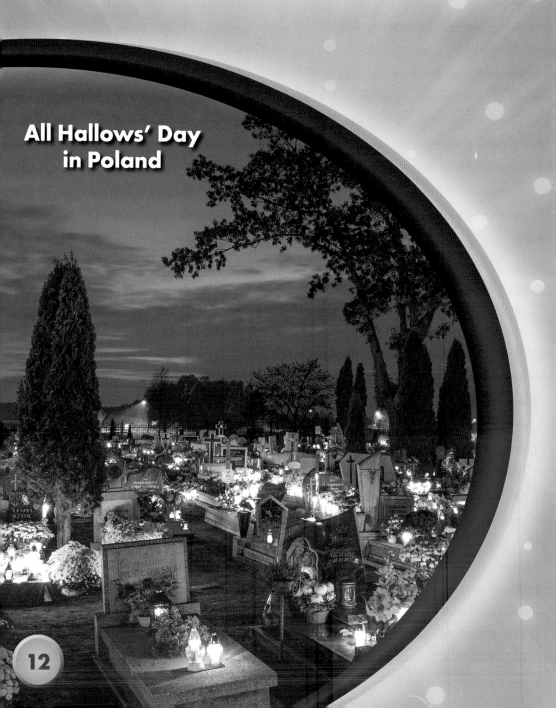

All Hallows' Day in Poland

How Do You Say?

Word	Pronunciation
Celtic	KEL-tik
Samhain	SAOW-in

The night before was for loved ones who had died. It was called All Hallows' Eve. This night turned into Halloween.

Halloween is on October 31. Trick-or-treating and parties are usually done at night.

These activities can be
scary after dark!

Long ago, many children played **pranks** on Halloween.

Today, people give out more treats than tricks! They put up decorations to welcome children.

Families **carve** pumpkins.
This tradition came from
Ireland. People placed the
jack-o'-lanterns in front of
houses to keep ghosts away.

Make a Felt Jack-o'-lantern

You can cut out many shapes to make several different jack-o'-lantern faces!

What You Need:
- orange, green, black, white, and yellow felt
- pen or marker
- scissors and glue

What You Do:

1. Trace a large pumpkin shape on the sheet of orange felt. Cut it out.
2. Cut a stem shape out of the green felt. Glue it to the top of the pumpkin.
3. Draw jack-o'-lantern eyes, noses, and mouths on the other felt pieces.
4. Carefully cut out the shapes.
5. Use the shapes to create jack-o'-lantern faces on the felt pumpkin.

1

4

3

5

Some people have parties and bonfires. They bob for apples and drink apple cider.

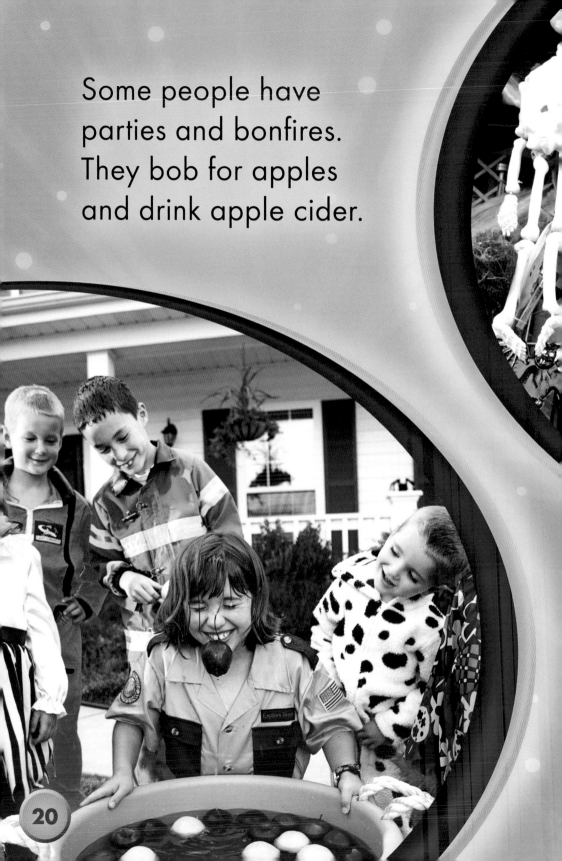

Others visit haunted houses and watch scary movies. People enjoy getting spooked on Halloween. Boo!

Glossary

carve—to cut a shape out of something

Celtic—relating to a group of early European people including the Irish and Scottish

Christians—people who believe in the teachings of Jesus Christ and the Christian Bible

festival—a celebration

jack-o'-lanterns—lit pumpkins with faces or designs cut into them

pranks—playful tricks

saints—people honored by Christians for their good deeds

traditions—customs, ideas, and beliefs handed down from one generation to the next

To Learn More

AT THE LIBRARY

Jones, Theodore. *Halloween's Spooky History*. New York, N.Y.: Gareth Stevens Publishing, 2016.

Lee, Sally. *A Short History of Halloween*. North Mankato, Minn.: Capstone Press, 2016.

Sebra, Richard. *It's Halloween!* Minneapolis, Minn.: Lerner Publications, 2017.

ON THE WEB

Learning more about Halloween is as easy as 1, 2, 3.

1. Go to www.factsurfer.com.

2. Enter "Halloween" into the search box.

3. Click the "Surf" button and you will see a list of related web sites.

With factsurfer.com, finding more information is just a click away.

Index